Original title:
Moonlit Mischief and Dreamy Delights

Copyright © 2024 Creative Arts Management OÜ
All rights reserved.

Author: Liam Sterling
ISBN HARDBACK: 978-9916-90-490-9
ISBN PAPERBACK: 978-9916-90-491-6

Whirls of Fantasy Under Cosmic Light

In the night where dreams take flight,
Stars whisper secrets, pure and bright.
Galaxies spin in an endless dance,
Inviting all to take a chance.

The moon weaves tales of ancient lore,
While comets blaze, a fleeting score.
With every twinkle, a wish is born,
In the vastness, our hearts are worn.

Nebulae bloom in colors rare,
Filling our souls with stardust air.
Planets glow in their cosmic race,
Creating beauty in boundless space.

In this realm where fantasies soar,
We find the magic we can explore.
Under cosmic light, we play and dream,
In whirls of wonder, life's a gleam.

Chasing Shadows in Dreamscapes

In the twilight, whispers call,
Footsteps trace, where shadows fall.
Fragments dance in midnight's glow,
Chasing dreams we hardly know.

Veils of mist and silver light,
Guide our hearts through endless night.
Onward through the maze we tread,
Finding paths where none have led.

Echoes of a Midnight Mirage

Beneath the stars, we wander lost,
Echoes fade, but never tossed.
Mirages flicker in the haze,
Luring hearts through endless maze.

Whispers float on gentle air,
Promises of dreams laid bare.
In the silence, secrets bloom,
Shadows dance within the gloom.

Glimmers in the Night's Embrace

Softly shine, the glimmers bright,
Guiding souls through velvet night.
In each twinkle, stories gleam,
Life's reflections, like a dream.

Wrapped in night's tender care,
Stars align, a cosmic flare.
Moments caught in fleeting sight,
Hope ignites within the night.

The Silhouette of Forgotten Fantasies

In the corner of the mind,
Silhouettes of dreams entwined.
Whispers of what once could be,
Lingering in memory.

Chasing visions lost in time,
Echoes soft as distant chime.
Fantasies that fade away,
Yet they linger, still they stay.

Mischievous Echoes of the Night

Underneath the silver moon,
Whispers tease, a sweet cocoon.
Footsteps dance on cobbled stone,
Echoes laugh; they're not alone.

Shadows stretch with playful glee,
Echoing the night's decree.
In the dark, where spirits play,
Mischief rules until the day.

Dreamscapes on the Edge of Reality

In twilight's glow, visions sway,
Where dreams and waking worlds display.
A fleeting glimpse, a dreamy flight,
Reality blurs in soft twilight.

Colors blend, and time stands still,
Heartbeats merge with cosmic thrill.
Each thought a spark, each breath a chance,
In this realm, we weave our dance.

Night's Whispers and Playful Pranks

The night winds carry secrets low,
Whispers flit, where shadows grow.
Stars twinkle with a knowing grin,
Playing tricks beneath the skin.

A rustling leaf, a distant sigh,
The playful night won't let us lie.
Mysteries lurk and spirits tease,
In a world where worries freeze.

Twinkling Games of Shadows

Flickering lights in the hush of night,
Shadows dance in a playful flight.
Moonbeams draw a path so bright,
Together we embrace the sight.

Footsteps soft on a gravel lane,
Twinkling games where laughter reigns.
In the dark, our secrets blend,
As night unfolds, and we transcend.

A Journey Through Celestial Dreams

Beneath the starry blanket wide,
We sail on whispers, side by side.
The moonlight guides our gentle sway,
As night unfolds, we drift away.

In cosmic hues, the galaxies gleam,
Each heartbeat pulses, a timeless dream.
Through nebulous clouds, we softly glide,
In this embrace, our souls reside.

The Twilight Revelry of Slumber

As shadows dance in dusky light,
The world transforms, sweet dreams take flight.
With every sigh, the veil draws near,
In twilight's glow, we shed our fear.

The whispers of night weave tales untold,
In velvet depths, our wishes unfold.
We lose ourselves in magic's weave,
In slumber's arms, we truly believe.

Fantasies Wrapped in Veils of Night

In the stillness, secrets stir,
Wrapped in whispers, shadows blur.
Fantasies twirl on gossamer wings,
As night unfurls, the silence sings.

The stars above, like distant dreams,
Illuminate paths in silver beams.
We chase the thoughts that softly tread,
In veils of night, they dance, they spread.

Mischief Among the Silhouetted Trees

In twilight's arms, where shadows play,
The trees conspire, in secret sway.
Soft laughter echoes, a playful tease,
As mischief brews among the trees.

With rustling leaves, the night takes flight,
They whisper tales of daring night.
We join their dance, the world at ease,
In joyful chaos, among the trees.

Enigmatic Adventures Beneath the Stars

In the velvet sky, secrets dwell,
Whispers of journeys, tales to tell.
With each twinkle, a story unfolds,
Mysteries woven in silver and gold.

Footsteps echo on the soft, cool grass,
Dreams awaken as shadows pass.
Through the night, the cosmos gleams,
Guiding us softly to distant dreams.

Starlit Puzzles of the Heart

Puzzle pieces scattered wide,
Underneath the stars we confide.
Every glance a riddle inspired,
In the light of the moon, our hearts desired.

We trace the constellations' flow,
Searching for answers in the glow.
With each heartbeat, connections spark,
Starlit journeys ignite a new arc.

Laughter in the Gloaming's Grasp

As dusk descends, laughter takes flight,
In the gloaming, the world feels right.
Echoing joy through the softening air,
Moments suspended, free from despair.

Flickering lights in the twilight shine,
Every smile weaves a wavering line.
Together in echoes, we dance and weave,
Building memories that never leave.

A Tapestry of Nightly Whispers

In the tapestry of night, whispers entwine,
Secrets of stars in a dance so divine.
Every sigh tells a story profound,
In the silence, our dreams are unbound.

With starlight's glow, hearts intertwine,
In the darkness, our souls combine.
A mosaic of dreams, in shadows we find,
Nightly whispers, forever aligned.

The Spellbinding Hour of Enchantment

In twilight's hush, the shadows dance,
With whispered tales of a fleeting glance.
Stars awaken, shimmering bright,
Casting dreams through the velvet night.

A soft breeze stirs the silent trees,
Carrying secrets upon the breeze.
Moonlight weaves through the darkened air,
A magical spell, beyond compare.

Crickets sing a lullaby sweet,
Underneath where the earth and sky meet.
In this hour, the heart feels free,
Entwined in the charm of mystery.

Time suspends in a gentle embrace,
As enchantment unveils its tender grace.
In this realm where wonders abide,
The soul dances, with nothing to hide.

Adventures in the Stolen Glow

Chasing shadows in the golden light,
Mapping dreams that take to flight.
Fields of wonder beckon near,
In stolen moments, joy appears.

With footsteps soft on the dewy ground,
A magic path where dreams are found.
Whispers echo through the trees,
Carried high upon the breeze.

The glow ignites a spark within,
A journey where the heart can spin.
Each adventure, a tale to unfold,
In the warmth of magic, bright and bold.

Underneath the starlit skies,
We chase the dawn, where freedom lies.
Through the wild and woven flow,
We script our fate in the stolen glow.

Fancies Swaying in the Night Air

Beneath the moon's gentle embrace,
Fancies sway with delicate grace.
Stars wink softly, velvet dreams,
Drift in currents of silver beams.

The night whispers secrets untold,
Of shimmering tales and hearts of gold.
In the shadows, our hopes take flight,
Dancing boldly through the night.

Winds carry laughter, sweet and light,
Spinning fancies that spark delight.
Each flicker of light paints the dark,
Igniting the soul, a vibrant spark.

Time holds its breath in this enchanted hour,
As we bloom like a midnight flower.
In tranquility, our spirits soar,
Swaying gently, forevermore.

The Melodies of Molten Dreams

In the silence where echoes play,
Molten dreams softly sway.
Harmony flows like a gentle stream,
Crafting worlds from a heartfelt dream.

Notes entwine in a rhythmic dance,
Awakening hearts to a timeless romance.
Every heartbeat sings a tune,
Beneath the watchful silver moon.

Melodies linger in the twilight air,
Whispering wishes with tender care.
Each note a promise, a wish set free,
In this symphony of mystery.

Through each verse, our souls unite,
In the glow of dreams, we take flight.
Together we weave the evening's song,
In the harmony where we belong.

The Mischievous Stars Play

In the velvet night they dance,
Twinkling with a cheeky glance,
Whispers of secrets they relay,
The mischievous stars at play.

They toss their light like a game,
Chasing shadows, never the same,
In laughter, they twirl and sway,
The mischievous stars at play.

Above the world, they laugh and cheer,
Guiding lost souls who wander near,
With a wink and a glimmer's ray,
The mischievous stars at play.

They call to the moon, soft and bright,
Spinning tales of pure delight,
In the quiet night's ballet,
The mischievous stars at play.

Serenade of the Nocturnal Breeze

Whispers of night softly sigh,
As the cool breeze wanders by,
Rustling leaves in gentle tease,
A serenade of the nocturnal breeze.

Under the glow of the pale moon,
Nature hums a soothing tune,
Stars above sway with such ease,
A serenade of the nocturnal breeze.

Carried secrets from afar,
Echoes of dreams beneath a star,
In the hush, the heart finds peace,
A serenade of the nocturnal breeze.

With every flutter, shadows dance,
In harmony, they take their chance,
To lose themselves as sighs release,
A serenade of the nocturnal breeze.

Tales from the Twilight Garden

In the garden where shadows blend,
Softly, the day starts to end,
Flowers whisper tales so sweet,
From the twilight garden, they greet.

Crickets sing as the sun dips low,
Guiding light with their soft glow,
Underneath the stars that meet,
From the twilight garden, they greet.

Secrets linger in the air,
Stories woven with gentle care,
Every petal holds a heartbeat,
From the twilight garden, they greet.

In the hush of dusk's embrace,
Night unfolds with gentle grace,
Magic blooms where dreams compete,
From the twilight garden, they greet.

Laughter Under the Cosmic Canopy

Beneath the stars, our hearts collide,
In joy, we let our spirits ride,
Galaxies twinkle, our dreams unfasten,
Laughter under the cosmic canopy.

The universe hums a playful tune,
While planets spin and comets swoon,
In twinkling jest, hidden charms fashion,
Laughter under the cosmic canopy.

Moonbeams kiss the earth's sweet face,
We dance in this celestial space,
Where every heartbeat finds its passion,
Laughter under the cosmic canopy.

With every wish upon a star,
Together, we find who we are,
In the night's magic, hearts in fashion,
Laughter under the cosmic canopy.

Nighttime Revelries in the Glimmering Glow

Underneath the silver moon,
Whispers dance like soft balloons.
Shadows play in fading light,
Dreams awaken, taking flight.

Laughter echoes through the trees,
Carried gently by the breeze.
Stars twinkle with a playful wink,
In this world, we barely blink.

Moonlit paths invite our feet,
Every heartbeat, soft and sweet.
Moments twirl like autumn leaves,
In this night, our spirit weaves.

Glimmers spark in eyes so bright,
In revelries of pure delight.
Together, we will always roam,
In this glow, we find our home.

Ethereal Laughter Beneath the Cosmic Veil

Beneath the sky, vast and wide,
Ethereal laughter, side by side.
Galaxies spin, swirling grace,
In this dreamlike, endless space.

Nebulas shimmer in hues divine,
Painting joy with every line.
Echoes of mirth, sweet and free,
Woven in the cosmic sea.

Stars whisper secrets, old and wise,
Filling the dark with bright surprise.
Every twinkle tells a tale,
Of love that journeys through the veil.

As we dance in starlit glow,
Hearts unbound, we come and go.
In this realm where laughter reigns,
Freed from worries, lost in gains.

Secrets Unraveled in the Softest Night

In the hush of twilight's grace,
Secrets gather, face to face.
Under stars, we softly sigh,
Whispers travel, low and high.

The night's embrace, a tender cloak,
Each word cherished, gently spoke.
In the dark, our truths align,
Bound by the warmth of the divine.

Velvet skies with stories bright,
Bathed in the gentle, silver light.
Here, the universe unfolds,
With every secret, love beholds.

Through shadows deep and colors rare,
In this space, we freely share.
Moments captured, hearts at peace,
In the night, our fears release.

Serenade of Starlight and Tea-Time Tricks

A teacup clinks in soft delight,
As starlight sprinkles the night.
Brewing dreams with every sip,
In this moment, we lose our grip.

With every laugh, we share a spell,
Echoing magic, all is well.
Tea-time tricks with hearts so true,
In quiet joys, we start anew.

Stars blink down, a guiding light,
Leading us through the velvet night.
With every act, our spirits soar,
In this serenade, we find more.

Together we weave tales and cheer,
Each sip shared brings us near.
In laughter, love, and starlit play,
We weave our dreams till break of day.

Lullabies for the Wandering Soul

In twilight's embrace, dreams softly heed,
Stars twinkle gently, where shadows lead.
Whispers of night call the weary in,
Restless hearts find solace, let peace begin.

Each sigh of the breeze cradles the day,
Guiding lost spirits, they drift away.
Moonlight like silver, a tender caress,
Lullabies murmur, offering rest.

The road may be long, yet hope's light stays,
In the depths of night, the spirit sways.
Cradled by darkness, they wander free,
Softly embracing what we cannot see.

Beneath the Astral Canvas

Beneath the stars, a tapestry gleams,
Infinite wonders, woven in dreams.
Galaxies twirl in a cosmic waltz,
Painting the sky with celestial vaults.

Constellations whisper stories of old,
Of heroes brave and treasures untold.
The universe hums a melodic tune,
Guiding our hearts by the light of the moon.

Fleeting moments caught in time's gentle sway,
Under the heavens, we ponder and play.
Dreams intertwine with the stars high above,
Beneath the astral canvas, we find our love.

A Wisp of Nighttime Enchantment

A wisp of twilight dances in flight,
Glimmering softly, a breath of the night.
Moonbeams weave magic in shadows so deep,
Where secrets are kept, and dreams often seep.

The woods brim with whispers of tales untold,
With echoes of laughter from days of old.
Crickets serenade with a soothing refrain,
As stars sprinkle laughter, like soft summer rain.

Enchantment unfolds with a flicker of light,
Inviting the hearts that roam in the night.
In this veiled moment, magic ignites,
A wisp of wonder, beneath quiet sights.

Celestial Riddles in the Dark

In the silence of night, riddles arise,
Hidden in shadows, veiled by the skies.
Stars hang like jewels, a cryptic display,
Whispering secrets the cosmos convey.

What lies beyond in that infinite sphere?
Questions unanswered, yet calling us near.
Black holes and comets, the dance of the spheres,
Echoing softly through time and through years.

Each twinkle, a puzzle, each shimmer, a key,
Unlocking the mysteries of what's yet to be.
In the vastness of dark, light flickers and grows,
Celestial riddles, where wonder flows.

Euphoria in Silver Reflections

In the moon's bright glow, we swirl and glide,
Mirror of dreams on the silver tide.
Laughter dances in the gentle breeze,
Whispers of joy flutter through the trees.

Stars unveil secrets in the night air,
Magic surrounds us, vibrant and rare.
Each moment a spark, igniting the heart,
In this realm of wonder, we'll never part.

Ripples of peace in a tranquil sea,
Unified souls in perfect harmony.
As shadows depart and the dawn draws near,
We'll chase the light, free from all fear.

Euphoria rises like a swift flame,
In silver reflections, we'll play the game.
Together we'll weave a tapestry bright,
In the heart of the night, we find our light.

Night's Playground of Fantasia

Underneath the velvet sky so wide,
Dreams take flight on this whimsical ride.
Beneath starlit canopies, hearts entwine,
In a playground where shadows brightly shine.

Fireflies whisper in secrets they hold,
While laughter blooms like marigold.
Each corner turned, a wonder unfolds,
In this realm of fantasy, stories are told.

The moon casts spells, a magical sway,
Guiding us through this vibrant ballet.
Every twinkle a promise, every sigh,
In the dance of adventures, we'll soar high.

Night's playground sings in silvery tones,
Where echoes of joy and love are sown.
We'll wander through dreams, hand-in-hand tight,
In the embrace of the enchanting night.

The Dance of Dusk and Delirium

As the sun dips low, colors start to blend,
A canvas of chaos that will not end.
Waves of twilight wash over the land,
In the grip of delirium, we take a stand.

Footsteps echo where shadows play,
In this dance of dusk, we find our way.
Each heartbeat a rhythm, wild and free,
Lost in the moment, just you and me.

Whispers of night invite us to sway,
The stars join the chorus, brightening gray.
With every swirl, we break all the norms,
In this fleeting bliss, passion transforms.

The dusk holds mysteries wrapped tight in night,
A vibrant allure that tells of our plight.
Let's dance till dawn breaks, hearts intertwined,
In the embrace of delirium, love defined.

Secrets Woven by Twilight

As twilight descends, secrets take flight,
Threads of dreams spun in the dimming light.
Cloaked in soft whispers, the shadows may weave,
Tales of the heart that we dare to believe.

Stars peek through curtains of velvety night,
Guardians of stories bathed in their light.
Each twinkle a hint of wonders untold,
In the hush of the dusk, magic unfolds.

Through sighs and sweet laughter, we dance in time,
Chasing the echoes, heartbeats in rhyme.
With every shared glance, our fates intertwine,
In secrets woven, we find the divine.

Twilight, a tapestry, rich in its hues,
Holds mysteries lingered like soft evening blues.
Together we'll cherish each moment we find,
In the realm of the night, souls gently aligned.

Mischievous Glances Through Velvet Clouds

Veiled in mist, the moonlight glows,
Whispers hide where the cool wind blows.
Dreams awaken, dance in sight,
Mischief twinkles in the night.

Gentle shadows play their game,
Innocent laughter, never the same.
A spark of joy within the haze,
Glances exchanged, a silent praise.

Each moment shimmers, bright and bold,
Tales of wonder waiting to be told.
With every stir and playful shroud,
Hearts unite through velvet clouds.

Secrets Spiraled in a Celestial Dance

Stars align in perfect time,
Veils of night, a soft sublime.
Each twinkle holds a tale untold,
Secrets spiral, brave and bold.

Galaxies twine in cosmic grace,
Whispers glide through endless space.
Revelations wrapped in light,
Dance of shadows, dark and bright.

Moonbeams kiss the earth so rare,
A silent pact, a cosmic flair.
In every spin, the heartbeats rise,
Secrets held in starry eyes.

Soft Serenades of Twilight Tales

In soft twilight, the world slows down,
Whispers of dusk in a golden gown.
Crickets sing their lullabies,
While the sun dips in peachy skies.

Gentle breezes weave through trees,
Carrying tales like autumn leaves.
Rustling memories softly blend,
Each note a comfort, a cherished friend.

Woven stories of day now past,
Moments linger, gradients cast.
As night unfolds its dusky veil,
We find our peace in twilight tales.

Stardust Frolics on a Blanket of Night

Softly the stars begin to shine,
Scattered jewels on a canvas divine.
Stardust whispers, dreams take flight,
Frolicking in the heart of night.

Wandering souls in playful embrace,
Chase the echoes of cosmic grace.
Every twinkle, a wink of fate,
Dancing freely, patiently await.

Through the cosmos, laughter swirls,
A ballet of light, the universe twirls.
On this blanket where shadows play,
Frolic in stardust, night's ballet.

Echoes of Laughter on the Breeze

Children run wild, chasing light,
Giggles and whispers take flight.
The sun sets low, casting gold,
In this moment, joy unfolds.

Soft breezes carry their cheer,
As shadows dance, drawing near.
Fleeting moments, sweet and bright,
Laughter echoes into the night.

The Dance of Eclipsed Illusions

Under a moon that's veiled in shade,
Dreams and whispers serenade.
Figures twist in the dimmed glow,
Where truth and fantasy flow.

Layers of thought intertwine,
In a waltz, both yours and mine.
Fractured visions play their part,
A ballet of the hidden heart.

Nightfall's Whimsical Adventures

As twilight spills its inky hue,
The stars awaken, bright and new.
Wandering souls twirl in delight,
Chasing the dreams of the night.

Fires crackle, stories unfold,
Mysteries wrapped in warmth's hold.
Elfin laughter, a sweet refrain,
Guides us through the evening rain.

In Pursuit of Starlit Secrets

With every step on the soft grass,
Whispers beckon, daring us to pass.
The night sky twinkles, secrets to share,
A cosmic dance, beyond compare.

Winds carry tales from ages past,
In the silence, shadows cast.
We chase the stars, we seek the lore,
In the vast expanse, we want more.

Whimsy in the Ether's Embrace

In twilight's gentle sigh, they play,
With dreams that dance and drift away.
The stars whisper secrets on the breeze,
Where laughter floats among the trees.

Clouds wear colors, vivid and bright,
Painting the canvas of the night.
Creatures of light ambush the dark,
Chasing shadows with joy and spark.

Echoes of giggles intertwine,
In the ether's web so fine.
Every moment, a fleeting chance,
To join in the whimsical dance.

In this realm, where wishes roam,
Hearts find a warmth, a cherished home.
Embraced by wonder, love takes flight,
A tapestry woven from pure delight.

The Celestial Feast of Imagination

Under the swell of a starlit dome,
Ideas bloom, and thoughts find home.
An endless feast of dreams unspooled,
Where every whimsy is lovingly fueled.

Galaxies swirl in colors so bold,
Stories untold begin to unfold.
With cosmic spices, each vision flows,
As creativity's river ceaselessly grows.

Tables of clouds, with laughter to share,
Bounties of joy fill the midnight air.
Chimeras of thought, on silver plates,
Entice the heart as the mind celebrates.

In this banquet of the divine,
Imagination reigns as we dine.
Together we sip the starlit brew,
As visions dance in vibrant hue.

Nocturnal Wonders Under Festival Skies

Beneath the canopy of a velvet night,
Flare fireworks burst in dazzling light.
Each spark a whisper, a joyful song,
Guiding the dreamers where they belong.

Lanterns afloat in a sea of stars,
As magic travels both near and far.
With laughter ringing through the air,
Nocturnal wonders awaken a flare.

Children twirl in their colorful dreams,
While the moonlight weaves silver beams.
The night, a canvas ripe for play,
Where joy ignites and fears decay.

Under this sky, we find our way,
In the embrace of night's ballet.
Together we dance with twinkling eyes,
Caught in the spell of festival skies.

Luminous Chimeras in the Dusk

As dusk descends with a tender kiss,
Chimeras dance in a state of bliss.
Shadows meld with the fading light,
In a realm where day gives way to night.

Flickering softly like firefly dreams,
Colors entwine in silken gleams.
Creatures of wonder begin to play,
In the twilight spells where shadows sway.

These visions rise in delicate flight,
Breathing enchantment into the night.
Each whispering breeze carries tales anew,
Of luminous chimeras that wander through.

In this gentle blend of dusk and glow,
We find the magic that weaves and flows.
Here in the hush, our spirits ignite,
Amongst the chimeras, pure delight.

Fables Woven in Shadows

In twilight's grasp, tales arise,
Whispers of truth, beneath the skies.
A world of secrets, hidden and bright,
Each fable woven, in shadowed light.

A fox in cunning, a hare in flight,
Lessons of wisdom, in day and night.
Nature's own canvas, painted so bold,
Stories of ages, in silence told.

Beneath the willows, a dance of time,
A murmur of magic, a song's soft chime.
Embracing the mystery, we turn the page,
In the heart of the forest, we find our sage.

So gather 'round, let the stories flow,
In the gentle dark, where dreams will grow.
For every shadow, a light will gleam,
In fables woven, we learn to dream.

The Allure of Dreaming Skies

Beneath the stars, where dreams take flight,
Horizons whisper in the soft twilight.
Clouds like pillows, floating so high,
The allure of freedom, in dreaming skies.

A path of starlight, shining so bright,
Guiding the wanderer through the night.
With every twinkle, a secret shared,
In the canvas of cosmos, souls are bared.

The moon, a muse, paints hopes anew,
Casting shadows in shades of blue.
Each heartbeat echoes, the universe sighs,
In the vast expanse of dreaming skies.

So lay your burdens, let worries cease,
In the gentle embrace of cosmic peace.
For every dreamer, a wish complies,
In the wonder and magic of dreaming skies.

Mystical Murmurs in the Moonshade

In moonlit glades, secrets entwine,
Whispers of owls, in rhythms divine.
Breeze through the branches, a soft serenade,
Mystical murmurs in the moonshade.

Footsteps of fairies on soft woodland floor,
Dancing through dreams, forevermore.
With every ripple of silver light,
Nature's own stories in the night.

The stars look down, with eyes of fire,
Igniting the heart with unknown desire.
Each flicker a promise, each shadow a sign,
In the embrace of the night, all is divine.

So let us listen, and wander far,
Guided by echoes of each twinkling star.
For in the stillness, where magic is laid,
We find the truth in the moonshade's aid.

Tales of Echoes and Nightingale's Song

In valleys deep, where echoes play,
Nightingales sing of another day.
Their melodies weave through trees so tall,
Tales of love and loss that enthrall.

Through rustling leaves, stories emerge,
A symphony of life, an endless surge.
With every note, a heart laid bare,
In whispers of song, we find our care.

The past dances lightly on the breeze,
Filling the air with sweet memories.
Each echo a promise, a timeless throng,
In the gentle embrace of nightingale's song.

So close your eyes and listen near,
For tales are waiting, soft and clear.
In every echo, a tale belongs,
In the heart of the nightingale's song.

Sway of the Enchanted Breeze

Whispers linger in the air,
Carried softly, light as prayer.
Dancing leaves in twilight's sheen,
Nature's song, a serenade serene.

Moonlight bathes the world in dreams,
Rippling soft like silken streams.
Every shadow sways and swirls,
Embracing night as magic unfurls.

Gentle breezes brush the trees,
Caressing flowers with such ease.
A symphony of rustling leaves,
The heart of night in quiet weaves.

In this realm where spirits play,
Nature's pulse, a soft ballet.
With every breath, the world appears,
A dance of joy beyond our fears.

Veils of Nighttime Whimsy

Stars peek through the velvet black,
A tapestry, no thread to track.
The moon, a lantern glowing bright,
Guides the dreams that take to flight.

Shadows wink beneath the trees,
Softly swaying with the breeze.
In the hush, a hint of glee,
Whispers share a mystery.

Laughter echoes far and near,
Creatures stir, the night draws near.
With every rustle, tales unfold,
In the warmth of night so bold.

Veils of magic cloak the ground,
In this haven, joy is found.
With each heartbeat, dreams ignite,
As the world embraces night.

Illusions Under the Starlit Veil

Glimmers dance on silver streams,
Illusions weave through whispered dreams.
Beneath a sky that's ink and pearl,
Magic swirls in every whirl.

Thoughts drift like clouds in the night,
Veiling truth in soft moonlight.
What is real, what is a game?
In the dark, it's all the same.

Listen close, hear laughter call,
Echoes beckon, rise and fall.
In this realm of shades and hues,
The heart untangles hidden clues.

A dance of dreams, a fleeting scene,
Illusions formed from what might have been.
With every breath, the fabric bends,
Under the stars where wonder sends.

Pantomime of the Night Creatures

In the dark, the echoes play,
Nighttime whispers, wild ballet.
Creatures dance in shadows deep,
With secrets that the night must keep.

Flickering eyes in soft moon's glow,
Guide the steps of tales we know.
Soft footfalls on the forest floor,
A symphony that asks for more.

Crickets chirp their melodic tune,
Singing praises to the moon.
With every beat, the night unfolds,
Stories lingering, yet untold.

In this pantomime of glee,
The world becomes a mystery.
Lost in wonder, we embrace,
The night creatures' playful grace.

Whispers of Silver Shadows

In the stillness of night, they call,
Hints of secrets whispered small.
Moonlit paths where shadows play,
Encounters veiled in soft decay.

Eclipsed echoes dance and sway,
Fleeting moments held at bay.
Through the mist, they beckon near,
A world unknown, both strange and dear.

Silver threads entwine the air,
Softly weaving tales they'd share.
With each sigh, a story shared,
In this realm, all hearts prepared.

So let the whispers guide the night,
Silver shadows, pure delight.
In the silence, find your song,
Where the lost and dreamers long.

Starlit Secrets on a Midnight Escapade

Beneath the stars, a journey starts,
With every twinkle, fluttered hearts.
The night unfolds its silken wing,
Unveiling dreams that twilight brings.

Each secret shared in hushed refrain,
In the moon's glow, love remains.
A dance of shadows, hands entwined,
In every glance, our fates aligned.

The universe spins, a lover's answer,
In starlit whispers, our souls shall dance here.
Navigating paths both old and new,
While the night sky brightens our view.

Embrace the magic, let it guide,
On midnight's ride, we shall reside.
In starlit secrets, fears will fade,
With memories made, our hearts untrayed.

Enchanted Reflections in Twilight Tides

As daylight wanes, the waters gleam,
Whispers of dusk weave through a dream.
Ripples carry tales of old,
Where secrets linger, brave and bold.

The horizon blushes with azure grace,
Nature's palette, a warm embrace.
Mirrored faces in the tide,
Reflections of love we cannot hide.

In twilight's kiss, the world turns gold,
Every heartbeat, a story told.
As shadows stretch, we take our flight,
In enchanted nights, we find our light.

Let the tide draw us ever near,
In its depths, we shed our fear.
With every wave, our spirits glide,
In twilight's embrace, side by side.

Celestial Pranks Under a Dazzling Canopy

Beneath the vast and twinkling sky,
Stars conspire, mischief awry.
With laughter dancing on the breeze,
They play their games with effortless ease.

Clouds drift in whimsical arrays,
Shaping dreams in playful ways.
Comets wink, a secret flight,
Weaving wonder into the night.

Galaxies twirl in cosmic glee,
Inviting us to join the spree.
With every spark, the heart ignites,
In this enchanting, endless night.

So let the cosmos paint our fate,
In celestial pranks, we celebrate.
Under this canopy so bright,
We dance like stars in pure delight.

Mystical Dancers on the Whispering Breeze

In the moonlight, shadows twirl,
Silent whispers start to swirl.
Leaves a-dance, a gentle tease,
Nature's grace upon the breeze.

Figures sway, ethereal light,
Dreamlike forms take graceful flight.
Traces soft, like silk they weave,
In the dark, they never leave.

Stars applaud from far above,
Witnessing this dance of love.
Time stands still as spirits glide,
On the wind, they do abide.

Each step speaks of ancient lore,
As they summon from the core.
In the night, their magic thrives,
Mystical are these dancers' lives.

Fanciful Dreams in a Gilded Sky

Clouds like candy, soft and bright,
Swirling visions in the light.
Painted hues of pink and gold,
Fanciful dreams, a tale untold.

Gossamer threads in twilight soar,
Whispers float from shore to shore.
On the breeze, old wishes climb,
In this realm, there's no time.

Creatures born from pure delight,
Dance on beams of fading light.
In the dusk, they come alive,
In this space, we all can thrive.

Hearts are lifted, soaring high,
In a world where dreams defy.
Magic glows through every sigh,
Fanciful dreams in gilded sky.

Glimmers of Nightfall and Playful Whimsy

Twinkling stars, a playful sight,
Glimmers dance in the velvet night.
Laughter echoes, soft and free,
Whimsy blooms from memory.

Moonbeams play on gentle streams,
Woven threads of silver dreams.
Nature hums a lullaby,
To the wanderers passing by.

In this realm, the heart can sway,
Lost in wonder, come what may.
Hands reach out to touch the glow,
As the night begins to flow.

Trail of stardust leads the way,
Through the night till break of day.
Glimmers bright with every whim,
As we dance on the night's hymn.

Fantasies Floating on the Nocturnal Air

In the silence, dreams arise,
Floating softly 'neath the skies.
Whispers sweet of tales untold,
Fantasies in night's firm hold.

Velvet veils and shadows creep,
Through the dark, they start to leap.
Each breath brings a story near,
As the stars begin to cheer.

Figures twirl in mystic grace,
Searching for a timeless space.
In the air, they spin and sway,
Finding joy where night holds sway.

Hearts united, spirits blend,
On this dream, we can depend.
In the stillness, our souls dare,
Fantasies floating in the air.

Whimsical Whispers Beneath the Astral Body

Stars hum low in cosmic flight,
Words weave through the velvet night.
Softly bright, secrets unfold,
In the hush, whispers of old.

Celestial dance of time and space,
Fleeting dreams in a soft embrace.
Galaxies twinkle, hearts align,
Infinite wonders, yours and mine.

Nebulas swirl, colors collide,
In the silence, wishes reside.
Echoes of laughter, distant calls,
Underneath the astral thralls.

Voices merge with the starlit glow,
Carried by winds where wishes flow.
Beneath the vast, celestial sea,
Whimsical whispers, wild and free.

Chasing Dreams Through the Nebula's Gaze

Across the void, dreams take flight,
Guided by the nebula's light.
Hopes cascade like shooting stars,
Wandering hopeful, near and far.

Every spark a tale untold,
In the cosmos, brave and bold.
Floating softly, time stands still,
Chasing dreams through the quasar's will.

Celestial paths woven in grace,
Sculpted visions in endless space.
Whispers echo in the galactic haze,
Chasing dreams through the nebula's gaze.

Cradled by the cosmic breeze,
Hearts entwined like drifting leaves.
In the twilight, wishes ignite,
Chasing dreams into the night.

The Delicate Dance of Shadowed Wishes

In twilight's glow, shadows play,
Whispers of wishes softly sway.
Moonlit grace on a silken thread,
Where dreams flit and softly tread.

Each flicker holds a secret dear,
Woven in the fabric of fear.
In the silence, hearts will glean,
The delicate dance of what might have been.

Fleeting moments, a fleeting sigh,
Bathed in stars that shimmer and lie.
With every heartbeat, a wish takes flight,
Danced in shadows, lost to night.

Hold tight to dreams, let them float,
On gentle waves, like a boat.
In the dark, where wishes glisten,
Listen close to the shadows' mission.

Fae Flickers and Nightingale Songs

In moonlit glades, the fae do dance,
Twinkling lights in a playful chance.
Nightingales sing in soft refrain,
Melodies woven through the rain.

Flickers of magic spark the night,
Joyful laughter in pure delight.
Wings aflutter, whispers sweet,
Where harmony and mischief meet.

Underneath the arching trees,
Softly drifting on the breeze.
Tales of wonder through the throng,
Fae flickers and nightingale songs.

Embrace the beauty of twilight's grace,
Where dreams wander, a tranquil space.
In every corner, joy belongs,
With fae flickers and nightingale songs.

Tidal Dreams and the Play of Light

The tides whisper soft songs,
Beneath the moon's gentle glow.
Waves dance in fluid grace,
As dreams drift to and fro.

In the twilight's embrace,
Colors shimmer and blend.
Light paints the ocean's face,
A canvas without end.

Each ripple holds a tale,
Of distant shores untold.
Where dreams set their sail,
And hearts become bold.

We ride the ebb and flow,
In the night's tender light.
With the stars aligned so,
Our spirits take flight.

Illuminated Fantasies in Silken Shadows

Silken shadows softly sway,
In the glow of candlelight.
Whispers of the night play,
As dreams take gentle flight.

Glimmers of hope arise,
In the dance of flames so bright.
Illuminated by the skies,
Fantasies banish fright.

Every corner hides a tale,
Of mystery and delight.
Through the darkness, we sail,
Chasing the spark of night.

In this world of pure dreams,
We lose track of the hours.
Threads woven in moonbeams,
Life adorned with sweet flowers.

Whispers of the Silver Night

The silver night softly calls,
With voices from afar.
Underneath the blanket of stars,
Our hearts begin to spar.

Glistening dreams float high,
Like echoes on the breeze.
In the quiet, we sigh,
Finding calmness with ease.

Moonbeams dance on the lake,
Reflecting wishes made.
In the silence, the hearts ache,
Yet hope will never fade.

With whispers, we unite,
In the stillness we thrive.
In the shadows of the night,
In dreams, we come alive.

Secrets of the Starlit Sky

The starlit sky holds secrets,
In the depth of its embrace.
Dreams twinkle like bright tickets,
To a far-off, wondrous place.

Beneath the vast expanse,
We lay on fields of dreams.
In the moon's silver dance,
Life is more than it seems.

Each star tells a story,
Of love and loss and hope.
In this celestial glory,
Our spirits learn to cope.

With every glint, we sigh,
Finding solace in the night.
In the secrets of the sky,
We feel the world's pure light.

Midnight's Playful Serenade

Under a canopy of stars,
Whispers of the night begin,
Moonlight glimmers on the grass,
As shadows stretch and spin.

Laughter dances on the breeze,
A melody sweet and clear,
Time slips softly into dreams,
As night reveals its cheer.

Fireflies twinkle in a path,
Guiding footsteps, bright and free,
In this haven made of light,
We find our harmony.

The world outside fades away,
Here in midnight's warm embrace,
Every heartbeat feels like song,
In this enchanting space.

When Dreams Take Flight

In the hush of twilight's glow,
Imaginations start to soar,
Clouds become our ships of dreams,
Waves of wonder to explore.

Whispers call from distant shores,
With each sigh, a tale unfolds,
Magic weaves through sleepless nights,
As secrets gently unfold.

Across the sky, a painted brush,
Colors blend in twilight's art,
Every star a hope reborn,
As slumber claims the heart.

When dreams take flight, our spirits rise,
Free as birds from cage and care,
In this voyage of the mind,
We find the dreams we dare.

The Enigmatic Dance of the Night

Silhouettes sway in the dark,
A rhythm born of twilight sighs,
Within shadows, secrets stir,
As the moon embroiders the skies.

Eyes aglow with stories told,
Each glance holds a world anew,
Footsteps trace the paths of stars,
In this dance, the night bids adieu.

Curtains of velvet dusk unfold,
Stars shine bright in cosmic trance,
Every heartbeat weaves a tale,
As the night invites the dance.

Mysteries swirl like fog around,
In the silence, echoes play,
The enigmatic dance of night,
Carries souls until the day.

Celestial Revels in the Dark

When dusk drapes its shimm'ring veil,
The cosmos starts its play,
Stars ignite in ancient waltz,
As night unfolds its sway.

Galaxies twirl in spiraled grace,
Nebulas burst with vivid light,
Whispers of the universe,
Guiding dreams into the night.

Constellations tell of old,
Secrets kept from human eyes,
Each twinkle holds a promise bright,
In the deep, where wonder lies.

Celestial revels find their stage,
In shadows deep and wide,
The night reveals its splendor rare,
As starlit hearts abide.

The Curious Chronicles of Nightfall

Shadows stretch across the ground,
Whispers of secrets all around.
The moonlight glimmers on the leaves,
Nature's song, a lullaby that weaves.

Crickets chirp their nightly tune,
Beneath the watchful gaze of the moon.
Mysteries dance in the cool night air,
A tale unfolds with a gentle flare.

Stars twinkle like eyes in the dark,
Each one holds a story, a subtle spark.
Nightfall cradles dreams that soar,
In this quiet hour, we seek for more.

Together we wander, hand in hand,
In the depths of night, we make our stand.
The curious tales that nights impart,
Chanting the magic of the heart.

Secrets of the Dreamweaver's Art

In realms where dreams and shadows blend,
A weaver's touch, where journeys transcend.
Threads of silver, woven in flight,
Capturing wishes that glisten bright.

Softly brushed with hues of night,
Stories unfurl, a magical sight.
Imagination's brush paints the sky,
On canvas of stars, dreams flutter high.

Whispers of tales in slumber's embrace,
Echoes of laughter in a timeless space.
The dreamweaver's art, a spellbound dance,
Invoking a world where dreams find chance.

With every stitch, a heartbeat flows,
Secrets of life in the dreamer's prose.
Awake in the magic, let it impart,
The treasures hidden in the dreamweaver's art.

Stardust Trails of Fantastical Journeys

Beneath the stars, we start to roam,
With stardust trails leading us home.
Each step a story, every glance a spark,
In the vast expanse where dreams embark.

Galaxies spin in colors untold,
Magic and wonder, a sight to behold.
Through cosmic seas where wanderers thrive,
We ride the waves as our spirits dive.

Tales of courage and realms unseen,
Where hope and whimsy forever convene.
With hearts as our compass, we chase the light,
On stardust trails, we dance through the night.

In every heartbeat, the universe sings,
Carrying us forth on celestial wings.
Fantastical journeys await anew,
In the touch of stars, our dreams come true.

Enchanted Echoes in the Night's Caress

Under the veil of the night's soft grace,
Whispers of magic fill the space.
Echoes linger like a sweet refrain,
Calling us gently, again and again.

Moonlit paths lead to hidden glades,
Where stories await in the softly swayed.
The breeze carries secrets on feathered wings,
In the heart of night, enchantment sings.

Dreamers gather in the twilight glow,
Finding solace where the shadows flow.
Every heartbeat, a mystical sign,
In the night's caress, our souls align.

With every moment, the world seems bright,
Enchanted echoes guide us through the night.
In the silence woven with stars that bless,
We uncover the magic in night's caress.

Secrets Swaying on the Lunar Lullaby

Under the moon's gentle glow,
Whispers dance in the night,
Silent tales of the stars,
Wrapped in shadows so bright.

Luna's song calls to the heart,
Secrets unfold with the breeze,
Each note a soft, hidden part,
Floating through ancient trees.

Dreams drift on silvery beams,
In the calm of the dark sky,
Hearts are swayed by the dreams,
As the nighttime winds sigh.

A cradle for wishes, the night,
Holding hopes, gently pressed,
In the stillness, pure delight,
Where the deepest truths rest.

Echoes of Laughter in the Starlight's Embrace

Giggles ride the midnight air,
Carried through cosmic curves,
Eternal echoes of play,
Where the universe swerves.

In the twinkle of distant stars,
Laughter sparkles and glows,
Unseen bonds that reach afar,
In the rhythm of what flows.

Children of night paint their dreams,
In strokes of laughter and light,
With cheer that brightly beams,
They dance in the cloak of night.

Starlit whispers weave their tune,
Filling the sky with delight,
Where joy meets the silver moon,
In the embrace of the night.

Dreams Woven in Threads of Silver Light

In the fabric of the night,
Dreams are stitched with delicate grace,
Threads of silver shining bright,
Weaving every wish and trace.

Stars behave like skilled artisans,
Crafting wonders in air,
Each glimmer a fleeting chance,
To find solace and repair.

Fingers of light gently trace,
Patterns lost in the vast sea,
Embroidered in time and space,
Speaking of what's meant to be.

As dawn approaches with its hue,
Dreams fade softly, thin and slight,
Yet they bloom, and then renew,
In the threads of silver light.

Enigmatic Journeys in the Heart of Darkness

Within the heart where shadows dwell,
Journeys twist in whispered lore,
Mysteries hidden, stories swell,
In the depths, where spirits soar.

Footsteps echo on trails unknown,
Guided by the pulse of night,
Each heartbeat a seed that's sown,
In the absence of light.

Curiosity sparks the soul,
As darkness wraps in its embrace,
Seeking truth to make us whole,
In the shadows, we find our place.

With every step into the void,
Courage blooms in the dark's breath,
In this silence, we're deployed,
Charting maps beyond our death.

Luminous Mischief Painting the Night Sky

In the hush of dusk, they play,
Stars twinkle bright, a light ballet.
Whispers of cosmos swirl and glide,
Mischief in colors, they won't hide.

Galaxies spin in joyful spree,
Brushstrokes of light, wild and free.
They dance on clouds, a vivid sight,
Painting the canvas of the night.

With sparkling trails, their laughter rings,
Each twinkle crafted, a song that sings.
Through the dark veil, mysteries unfold,
Tales of the universe, shyly told.

As dawn approaches, they start to wane,
But echoes of magic will still remain.
In dreams they'll linger, forever bright,
Luminous mischief, painting the night.

Glowing Reveries in Hidden Groves

In whispering woods, where shadows creep,
   Glowing dreams awaken from deep.
  Moonbeams dance on leaves so rare,
   Enchanting warmth fills the cool air.

  Marshmallow clouds drift slowly by,
    Crickets hum a soothing sigh.
  Glimmers of hope play in the night,
   Nature's embrace, a cosmic light.

   Fireflies flicker like wishes cast,
    In secret groves, a spell is fast.
   Every twinkle, a story spun,
   Of ancient tales and gentle fun.

As dawn breaks soft, the glow subsides,
  But in our hearts, the magic bides.
 Hidden groves, in dreams, still stay,
   Glowing reveries, forever play.

Fluttering Spirits Beneath a Blanket of Stars

Spirits of night in gentle flight,
Beneath a blanket, woven tight.
With every flutter, a soft embrace,
Starlit whispers, a sacred space.

They dance through twilight, wild and free,
Glowing softly, a symphony.
In gardens of dreams where silence speaks,
Their laughter lingers, as daylight peaks.

Each star a beacon, a guiding light,
Spirits twirl in the soft twilight.
With moonlit graces, shadows entwine,
In endless dreams, their joys align.

As morning breaks, their songs will fade,
Yet forever in hearts, their essence laid.
Fluttering spirits, a joyful show,
Beneath the stars, love's gentle flow.

Wandering Hearts in the Cosmic Playground

Hearts that wander through realms untold,
In a cosmic playground, brave and bold.
With every wish, they take to flight,
Chasing nebulas, lost in light.

As comets streak with fiery tails,
They dance on dreams, where laughter sails.
With stardust trails beneath their feet,
Each moment a joy, a heart's heartbeat.

Across the galaxies, hand in hand,
Explorers of worlds, uncharted land.
With wonder found in every gaze,
They weave their stories in endless ways.

In the silence of night, they find their song,
Wandering hearts where they belong.
In the cosmic playground, love will reign,
Together forever, in joy and pain.

Enchantment Beneath the Glow

In the hush of twilight's charm,
Stars awaken, one by one.
Whispers echo, soft and warm,
Underneath the setting sun.

Golden rays begin to weave,
Stories wrapped in silken thread.
Nature sighs, as if to grieve,
For the day that gently fled.

Moonlit dreams begin to rise,
Casting shadows on the ground.
Filling hearts with sweet surprise,
In this magic, peace is found.

A dance of light, so divine,
Paints the sky in hues of grace.
In this moment, all align,
Bound together in this space.

Shadows Dance in Lunar Light

Silvery beams fall soft and light,
As shadows start to shift and sway.
In the calm of the night,
The moon holds court, come what may.

Branches whisper secrets low,
Beneath the stars, a timeless song.
In this ethereal glow,
The heart beats steady, strong.

Figures twirl in soft ballet,
Whirling dreams on gentle breeze.
Every pause, an art display,
Memories whispered through the trees.

Innocence captured by the night,
Hope unfurling, wide and free.
In shadows' twirl and lunar light,
A dance of souls, you and me.

A Night of Velvet Dreams

In the velvet cloak of night,
Dreams emerge like fireflies.
Glowing softly, pure delight,
Painting wonder in our eyes.

Waves of silence, gently crash,
Tides of thoughts drift in and out.
Whispers linger, hopes to clash,
In this sacred space, no doubt.

Nightingale sings from afar,
Softly threading through the air.
Underneath the morning star,
Magic dances everywhere.

Close your eyes and drift away,
On the clouds of starlit schemes.
Let the night make you its prey,
In the world of velvet dreams.

Dreamcatcher of the Celestial Realm

Beneath the weave of night's embrace,
Stars twinkle like a quilted sky.
In the dreamcatcher's gentle grace,
Wonders whisper, never shy.

Threads of fate that intertwine,
Crafting stories, tales unheard.
In this realm, your soul will shine,
With each flicker, hopes are stirred.

Floating worlds in twilight's span,
Where the dawn meets dusk's caress.
Here we dance, a cosmic plan,
Wrapped in love and boundless rest.

So let the dreams take flight anew,
In the embrace of starlit streams.
Awake refreshed, renewed, and true,
In the realm of endless dreams.

Milton Keynes UK
Ingram Content Group UK Ltd.
UKHW021928011224
451790UK00005B/61